REALLY, AREN'T ALL REAL ESTATE AGENTS THE SAME?

Donald Gorbach

Copyright © 2017 by Donald Gorbach

All rights reserved.

ISBN-10 1979190488
ISBN-13 978-1979190480

"IT'S NOT BAD THAT THERE ARE TOO MANY REAL
ESTATE AGENTS OUT THERE SELLING HOMES.
IT'S THAT THERE ARE TOO MANY BAD REAL ESTATE
AGENTS OUT THERE SELLING HOMES."

—ANONYMOUS

REALITYCOVERBOOKS.COM

www.ingramcontent.com/pod-product-compliance
Lightning Source LLC
Chambersburg PA
CBHW050214230526
45470CB00001B/377